Thanksgiving

Coloring Books For Kids

THIS BOOK BELONGS TO:

....

....

Gifted From: _______________________________

Happy
Friends
Giving

HAPPY
Friends
GIVING

Happy
Friends
Giving

Happy
Friends
Giving

HAPPY VEGAN
THANKSGIVING

Happy Vegan Thanksgiving

I'M A BREAST MAN

I'M A
BREAST MAN

MAKE
THANKSGIVING
GREAT AGAIN

MAKE
THANKSGIVING
GREAT AGAIN

MASTERBASTER

MASTERBASTER

MASTERBASTER

MOMMY & DADDY
are thankful for
ME!

MOMMY & DADDY
ARE THANKFUL FOR
ME!

POUR SOME
GRAVY
ON ME

POUR SOME
GRAVY ON ME

We are the
HAPPIEST
PUMPKINS
in the patch

I TEACH THE
CUTEST
PUMPKINS
IN THE PATCH

I'M JUST HERE FOR THE PIE!

I'M JUST HERE
FOR THE
PIE!

I'M THE CRAZY
Cat Lady

MY MOM
IS
MY
COSTUME

NANA
OF THE
PATCH

BOO!
BOO!
BOO!

SUGGESTED COLOR SOLUTION

HAPPY
Friends
GIVING

Happy
Friends
Giving

HAPPY VEGAN
THANKSGIVING

Happy
Friends
Giving

I'M A
BREAST MAN

Happy
Vegan
Thanksgiving

MAKE
THANKSGIVING
GREAT AGAIN

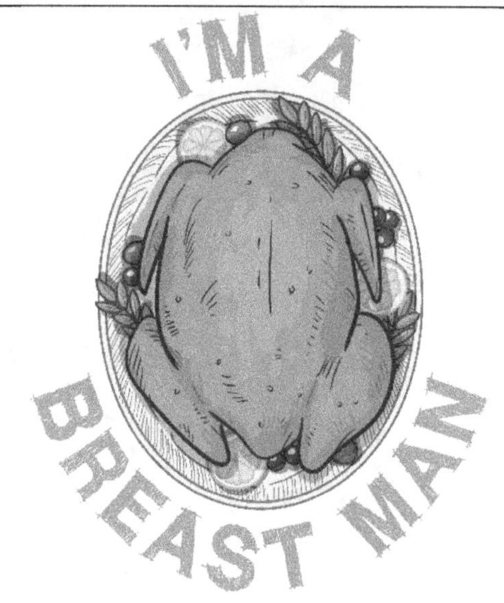

I'M A
BREAST MAN

MASTERBASTER

MAKE
THANKSGIVING
GREAT AGAIN

MASTERBASTER

MASTERBASTER

MOMMY & DADDY
ARE THANKFUL FOR
ME!

MOMMY & DADDY
are thankful for
ME!

POUR SOME
GRAVY ON ME

POUR SOME
GRAVY
ON ME

I TEACH THE
CUTEST
PUMPKINS
IN THE PATCH

We are the
HAPPIEST
PUMPKINS
in the patch

I'M JUST HERE
FOR THE
PIE!

BOO!
BOO!
BOO!